Being a Girl in Jieng Society

Dr Daniel A Mamer

A Note from the Publisher

The publisher wishes to acknowledge and thank Dr Douglas H. Johnson for his invaluable help and support for Africa World Books and its mission of preserving and promoting African cultural and literary traditions and history. Dr Johnson and fellow historians have been instrumental in ensuring that African people remain connected to their past and their identity. Africa World Books is proud to carry on this mission.

ISBN 978-0-6485028-9-0
© Daniel A Mamer, 2020

Published by Africa World Books Pty. Ltd.
(www.africaworldbooks.com)

Design and typesetting: Africa World Books

CHAPTER ONE

Introduction

There are sixty-six tribes or ethnic groups in the Republic of South Sudan. The Jieng tribe is the largest tribe in the country. The word Jieng, which the Nuer call Jang, means 'human,' as compared to other animals created by God. Like all African tribes, the Jieng tribe is a group of people who share a similar culture and a dominant language. Often, the term 'Jieng' is used interchangeably with 'Dinka,' but the people of the tribe prefer to be called Jieng, as 'Dinka' is a misnomer created by the British colonialists.

The Jieng tribe is subdivided into forty or fifty sections, each with a different name— Jieng tribe in Jonglei state is divided into four sub tribes namely: Hol, Nyarweng, Twi and Bor,in former Upper Nile Province, Rek, Agaar, Twic, Aliab, and so on in former Bhar-el-ghazal Preovince. Each of these sections has its own subdivisions. For example, Rek is further divided into Apuk, Giir Thik, Apuk Padoc, Apuk Juwiir, Thony, Kuac, and more. While different sections of the Jieng tribe vary slightly in dialect and cultural practice—this is called local specifics—they share one overarching language and culture.

Today, the Jieng tribe forms a little less than fifty percent of South Sudan's population. It is the biggest Nilotic tribe in South Sudan (all South Sudanese tribes are Nilotic, because they are all within the confines of the Nile basin or valley, a classification that is sometimes challenged). It is also the biggest Luo group in the whole of East Africa. In fact, it can be assumed that the Luo tribes of Kenya, Uganda, Tanzania, and possibly the DRC emigrated to those places from South Sudan.

The Jieng tribe is found in two of the former three provinces of South Sudan: Bhar-el-Ghazal and Upper Nile. The majority of Jieng people is found in the former Bhar-el-Ghazal province. Jieng homeland is a flat savannah grassland, like the Pampas in Central South America and the prairies in the United States, and is affected by floods at certain times of year. The grass that grows there is a particularly nutritious grass called Sudan grass, or *nuon lou* in Jieng language. When cattle eat this grass and apac, a common water plant in toic river networks, the cattle become very fat, have excellent health, and produce a lot of milk. This area is ideal for livestock rearing, making Jieng people among the biggest agropastoralists in Africa.

The Agaar community is one of the largest Jieng sections in the East-Central part of the former Bhar-el-Ghazal province, now called the Western Lakes State. The Lakes State is divided into three states: Yirol State, Gok State, and Western Lakes State. These states have also been subdivided administratively into counties, *payams*, and *boma*. Over ninety percent of the population of the Western Lakes State is Agaar. They call themselves Agaar-Madong,

The word Madong derives from dong, which is a common tree in the Western Lakes State area. The fruits of this tree are inedible, but the tree can be used for many other purposes, as its branches are very difficult to break, whether fresh or dry. Once upon a time, a few miles from Rumbek City, there lived an Agaar man called Malei. Malei lost a lot of goats and sheep to hyenas. Most Jieng build huts, or *tukls*, for their small ruminants (goats and sheep) or large huts called *luak* for all types of ruminants, including cattle. Malei built many different types of huts, some with strong walls made of thick mud, some with walls

4

made of timber, and some with walls of bamboo and mud. But hyenas broke through the walls however Malei built them and ate his goats and sheep.

To protect himself from further losses, Malei constructed a large hut/tukl using branches of dong. He twisted these branches so that they made a strong wall, firmly embedded in the ground without being plastered with mud. The door was made of similar material. The bottom of this fence was plastered with thick mud and chopped grass. One night, a hyena came and tried to enter the hut, which was full of goats and sheep, but it couldn't get in. By daybreak, defeated, hungry, and exhausted, the hyena sat on its hunches to watch the goats and sheep inside the hut. On and off, it began to dose. Malei knew that the poor animal was finished and defeated. As the red sun was about to surface from the east, Malei came out of his upstairs bedroom with a spear and saw the hyena. Though hyenas had eaten most of his goats and sheep in the past, Malei took pity on the animal. Instead of spearing it, he made a noise to alert it, and the hyena jumped up and ran towards the nearby forest.

The story of the dong tree symbolises the Agaar people's indomitable will and strength. This is an example of the ethnocentrism common to all human societies. Like all human cultures, the Agaar community creates its own mythologies and stories of possibility. From the legendary look of the hyena, the Agaar people coined the phrase '*Aci nyin ciet angune pane Malei*,' meaning 'You may come upon somebody whose looks of desire for something may be similar to that legendary look of the hyena that spent the night in the compound of Mr Malei, looking intently into the hut full of live goats and sheep it could not reach.'

Throughout this book, I will use my experience of being a girl in an Agaar community to represent the experience of being a girl in Jieng society at large, because all Jieng societies are culturally similar in their treatment of girls and women. The purpose of this book is to show not only how Jieng females are deprived of natural rights, but also how they are regarded as symbols of wealth. Most Jieng people, including women, refuse to accept the fact that women are mistreated by Jieng society, saying that the training and violence experienced by Jieng girls and women is for their own good and that of the society, but some do fight the system.

In this story, we will have two main characters. The first is an obedient young woman who we will call Abiola (pseudonym). Abiola accepts and follows the culture she lives in, representing the majority of Jieng girls, who follow the norms, values, and traditions of Jieng society. Our second main character is a girl revolutionary, who we will call Muona (pseudonym), representing those who have fought through the ages for their right to be respected. Muona is disliked by society, because she is fighting the system. We will see her struggle for success, ultimately failing.

There are only two periods in a girl's life when she is truly loved and respected. When girls are children under the age of ten, they are pampered and loved, learning light household duties from their mothers and being taught cultural norms such as language, tribal customs, and family and clan information. When girls become the grandmothers of their families, they again earn respect. They are addressed as 'Grandma' and hold great familial power.

Women suffer most in the period between childhood and old age, with this period lasting longer for women who marry young. In Jieng society, it is common for girls to be married off before they reach eighteen years of age, with girls sometimes settling into married life and motherhood at fourteen and fifteen years old. At this young age, birth complications are common, as girls' hips are not yet fully developed and medical facilities are scarce and of low quality. This frequently results in maternal deaths, rates of which are high.

There are eight chapters in this book, including this introduction, which introduces Jieng culture. Chapter two explores how Jieng culture welcomes girls in their early years, as well as the cultural training young girls receive. In chapter three, we discuss the training endured by girls in their adolescent years as they approach marriage, including punishments and beatings for disobedience. Chapter four discusses the married and maternal life of women, including instances of domestic violence. Chapter five explores the differing cultural roles of women and men, with women perceived as central social figures, yet stripped of freedom, while men are treated as leaders. Chapter six discusses how Jieng society and culture treats elderly women. Chapter seven discusses the impact and influence of contact with foreign cultures on Jieng culture. Chapter eight serves as a summary of this book.

In this book, we will see rising instances of violence against women since 1960. Why? Jieng culture has been influenced greatly by foreign ideas and practices (including alcohol consumption, which was far less prevalent in Jieng society before foreign influence intervened). Money, too, has influenced society, even in rural areas. Climate change has influenced food production, and farmers have been forced to sell livestock, especially cows, to close the food gap. Money has thus become increasingly important to food security and has perpetuated instances of violent domestic conflicts.

CHAPTER TWO

Early Childhood

Abiola and Muona were born on the same day in the same village as healthy baby girls and brought a lot of joy to their respective families. Abiola had three older brothers, while Muona had four. The arrival of the girls was celebrated by all the members of their families; their mothers were elated, because the girls were their only daughters. To their mothers, the girls were legacies, future women to train; to their brothers, they were sisters, who would one day get married and bring cows to the family; to their fathers, the girls were future ties to the important families from which their eventual spouses would hail—a daughter married into a well-respected family is a coveted social status symbol in Jieng societies.

At eighteen months of age, Abiola and Muona were weaned and taken to cattle camps by their grandmothers, where they stayed for a couple of years, drinking milk and occasionally eating sesame and peanut pastes, flour from grains and millets, and acida—porridge made thicker by adding more flour when cooking, usually eaten with vegetables and meat gravy, milk or milk butter, or *ghee*—brought from home by female relatives. These food items were irregular. The main foods in the cattle camps are milk and sometimes fish and wild meat, as there is a lot of game in the *toic*—a grassland area with very few isolated trees and bushes, usually flooded, where Sudan grass, or nuon lou, grows—where Jieng keep their cattle.

As they grew up, Abiola and Muona were loved by their relatives and called affectionate nicknames such as '*Nyan e wong*' and '*Nyan be hok chool*,' meaning 'The girl of the cows' and 'The girl who will repay the cows her mother was married with.' Throughout their childhood, the girls lived alternately in the village with their mothers and at the cattle camp.

By the age of five, the girls began to be introduced to domestic chores, like washing plates, sweeping the compound, fetching water for the family, and so on. By the age of ten, the girls were cooking, sweeping neatly, fetching firewood from the nearby forest or the cultivated fields, and taking food to the men, and they knew how to show respect to male relatives, bending or kneeling before them.

The girls were expected to be respectful and obedient. They were trained in culture and etiquette by their mothers. They were required to listen to and heed orders from their fathers and brothers without arguing.

If Abiola and Muona did not adequately perform one of their duties, they were scolded severely by their mothers, who demonstrated the correct way of completing tasks. If the girls did not follow their mother's instructions, their brothers beat them.

The girls were being moulded to fit predetermined positions in life. They were being taught to become good future housewives like their mothers, to always be obedient to their husbands, and to respect all males.

Some males in Jieng territory shirk agricultural work and stay in the cattle camps, leaving the cultivation of food crops to women and children, meaning that Abiola and Muona had to learn the art of cultivation much earlier in their lives. The women were responsible for almost all components that sustained livelihood, though this has changed slightly since the 1960s.

When Muona was thirteen years old, she began her first period.

Assuming she was sick, she rushed to her mother and told her what happened. The mother embraced her with great joy, much to her surprise. Muona's mother said '*Yin aci kuacm*,' meaning 'You now have reached puberty/maturity.' Muona had reached womanhood. In Jieng culture, this is a cause for great celebration. Women and girls from all over the neighbourhood assembled joyously and performed a women's dance called dany. Muona's mother informed her father of the great tidings. Her father brought a big bull to be slaughtered for the occasion, and there was a great feast.

Having reached this new phase of her life, Muona looked forward to officially taking over all the family's domestic chores, her mother now just a helping hand. Muona would learn to cook, clean, and perform all other household duties, which she would do for the family until she got married and started a family of her own.

Before taking over from her mother, Muona was put on a special diet for a period of six months. This diet included meat, fish, milk and milk products (such as *ghee*, or *mok e wong*), and vegetables, which are plenty in tropical zones. This feeding program was intended to help Muona gain the necessary weight to provide her with strength and a grown woman's appearance. Muona's clothing changed, now properly adhering to female dress traditions. To enhance her status, Muona now wore an elephant tusk on her left wrist, a symbol of high status in the community.

One of the most important ceremonies in Jieng celebrations of reaching womanhood is called *Akut e cin meec* or *kut e cin meec*, literally meaning 'Put the hands on fire.' This is a symbolic blessing of the young woman's hands, intended to ensure good cooking skills for the rest of her life. There are familial and societal fringe benefits for good cooks. On a familial level, if a man with several wives brings home rare food items, such as meat or fish, he takes these items to the house of the wife who is the best cook, where the largest share will remain, after giving other wives their shares. On a community level, if there is a community occasion, like a feast, where large quantities of food will be prepared, the women who are the best cooks are given the responsibility and honour of preparing the meal on behalf of the community.

Men do not talk about food much in Jieng communities, because food lovers are socially despised, but when young men are looking for wives, good cooking skills often factor into helping men and their families choose between two potential wives. Girls whose mothers are known to be good cooks find husbands more easily than those whose mothers are known to cook poorly.

Now that Abiola and Muona had matured, all the members of their families were watching their behaviour. Any violation of social norms, such as leaving their houses without good reason, talking to boys frequently, being lazy in carrying out domestic duties, or being rude, was severely punished by a beating from their brothers.

Most Jieng mothers spend a lot of time teaching their daughters how to be good, obedient housewives, and there are many rules and customs young girls must learn to adhere to. Husbands are not be looked in the eye or talked to, especially when they are angry. Meals must be regular and should be cooked before dark if food is available. A husband's visiting relatives must be well-received by his wife, who is expected to prepare sufficient meals for them and to care for them as her family. Meeting these expectations gives a woman the reputation of a good wife, and word of this status spreads throughout the area, earning respect and fame for her husband and herself.

One day, Muona was severely beaten at the cattle camp. Why? Each morning, cattle were released from their pegs to graze. The young calves remained in the cattle camp to graze nearby, while the very young calves were tied in the shade of huge trees. Muona, like other children her age, was expected to clean the area where the cattle were tied down and look after the calves. She had to remove the cow dung and spread it with a stick to dry, so that it could later be torched to provide heat and smoke, which would repel insects.

Muona had to provide soft grass and water for the tethered young calves, and she had to ensure that all of the calves, including those let loose to graze, were tethered in their usual places before the cows returned to the cattle camp at around 4.30 pm. After she had spread the dung to dry and moved the young calves to the shade, Muona went to swim in the river with the other children, forgetting all her duties. By the time she realised her mistake, it was too late. The older *calves* had met their mothers near the camp and suckled from them, meaning that the mother cows could not be milked that evening, leaving people hungry with no milk to drink; there was no other food available in the cattle camp.

On that day, Muona made a lot of mistakes. She didn't heap the dry dung or torch it to provide warmth and smoke, so the people were cold, and the insects were rampant. She didn't bring grass and water for the young calves, so the calves were hungry and thirsty. She didn't tie down the calves before their mothers arrived back at the camp, so they went to mothers and suckled them dry.

When Muona returned to the camp, she met her deranged brother, who gave her very severe beating with a cow's rope, leaving her aching and swollen. Muona was terribly sick for two days, laying on the ground.

Some of Muona's brother's friends blamed him for giving his sister such a severe beating, but they knew it was traditional to teach girls commitment to their duties and obedience to men, including their future husbands, in this way, so their scolding was not serious.

Like Muona, Abiola was undergoing rigorous training designed to turn her into an obedient wife and a good, loyal mother.

In Jieng culture, loyalty to the family is incredibly important. Divorce is not an option, because it affects the marriages of all family members. If a woman is divorced, her brothers will be also, because they use the cows given as bride price to their sister at her marriage to give to their own wives as bride prices. If the cows are taken away from their sister by her ex-husband and his family in the event of a divorce, they are taken from their wives by default (in order to repay the debt), and the relatives of their wives take their daughters and grandchildren back too. This means that women are expected to remain with their husbands no matter what.

In Jieng communities, daughters sometimes become sacrificial lambs for the benefit of their people, and this is considered the highest, most admirable honour. Boys, too, can act as sacrificial lambs to their communities, dying in defence of their territory when foreigners attempt to take the country, or when intruders want to harm or take away cattle, the most important Jieng asset.

CHAPTER THREE

The Adolescent Years and Marriage

Adolescence is a difficult time for all young people, and in Jieng culture, it is particularly dangerous for girls. During this time, mothers of teenage girls become very vigilant.

Today, Jieng people believe that girls must start their reproductive life as early as possible, allowing them time to produce more babies. Prior to the 1960s, however, Jieng culture allowed girls to grow to twenty or twenty-five years old before getting married. It was then thought that full maturity was necessary for healthy pregnancy, delivery, and motherhood. Girls were allowed to remain in their family homes until a man came to ask for their hand in marriage, so long as they did not elope.

Jieng girls can get married, sometimes, at the age of thirteen, and in rare cases, girls can be betrothed before entering puberty and sent to their husbands' houses to grow up with the promise that they remain untouched until maturity.

There is a traditional Jieng adage that says that 'Idleness is a devil's workshop.' To avoid encouraging idleness, most mothers ensure that their daughters are busy all the time, encouraging them to take over a wide range of household chores from a young age.

Unlike some other cultures, Jieng culture does not force girls to be accompanied by male relatives when travelling around their communities, so Jieng women and girls move freely and independently. They are warned to be cautious about strangers and exploitation, but they are trusted to protect themselves.

Many cultural norms and taboos exist to protect girls and women. For example, rape is culturally abhorred and is severely punishable. Perpetrators and their families find it difficult to get married, and in some cases, fights occur between families that result in everlasting injuries and death.

For the Agaar and Jieng people, family is a series of concentric circles of relatives—that is, circles with one centre. All families begin with a common ancestor, a centre, from and by whom offspring and ancestors are produced. These ever-widening circles become bigger and bigger until the population from one ancestor becomes so big that they form one clan with one totem. A number of clans can form a tribe if they are joined by a common ancestor(s). Similar concepts of family exist in other South Sudanese tribes and probably within tribes in other African countries.

Jieng communities take their family relationships, and associated vendettas, very seriously. If two unrelated families in a Jieng community fight and a member of one of the families is killed, a cycle of violence is likely to start. The youths of the grieving family meet to discuss a possible candidate from the perpetrating family to be killed in revenge, or vendetta, and the two families' respective clans become involved in the feud. In fact, if there is no young male representative in the perpetrating family, the victim family will choose the most handsome man from the perpetrating family's clan to kill and avenge their lost loved one's death.

To prevent vendettas from continuing indefinitely, there is a Jieng cultural value called blood compensation, or apuk e tir, meaning that something of value—a cow or cows, traditionally around thirty—

must be paid to the relatives of the deceased whose blood has been spilled. Paying compensation for someone killed by a family member requires a meeting of the first and second cousins and their nephews to establish how many cows each member of the perpetrating family should pay. Usually, the family's eldest brother or his own family pay the most, often eight to ten cows, while the rest of the cost distribution is determined by level of seniority. This compensation soothes the hearts of the relatives of the deceased and stops them from seeking further revenge.

If the man killed was unmarried, some of the paid cows are often used to marry him a wife. In Jieng culture, any brother of a deceased man, chosen by his family, can marry his brother's wife by proxy and produce children with her on his brother's behalf. Children born under these circumstances are his brother's legal children and are considered the nieces and nephews of their biological father. This practice, called ala hot, stems from the belief that all men have the right to have children, dead or alive, and is a cultural tradition that has existed for millennia in Jieng communities. It is now in danger of losing its significance under Western and religious influences, which demands that a man only marries one wife only and does not practise the idea of proxy marriages. The second reason of rejecting proxy marriages among the educated class staying in the urban areas is the economic pressure.

In traditional village settings, marrying on behalf of a lost brother was much less costly. The place-holding brother was to build a house for the wife of the deceased, and the wife was helped by her husband's relatives until her children matured. In village economy, the need for money was low, but the effect of climate change on agriculture and animal care has changed this. Today, educated people mostly stay in towns and urban areas, where regular income is needed for rent, electricity, water, food, clothing, education, and medical bills.

Jieng culture also shows the importance of relationships through sharing the benefits and burdens of family activities. For example, if a man is getting married, all his brothers, sisters, cousins, and nephews are expected to divide the bride price among themselves, with expected contributions ranging according to familial seniority. Marriage in some Jieng sections can be very expensive. In the Agaar area, bride prices generally range from thirty to four hundred cows.

When a Jieng girl marries, her family receives cows, usually between sixty and two hundred, but sometimes as few as twenty or as many as four hundred; in rare circumstances, girls may even be married for free. The cows are divided among the family members with the girl's direct family receiving the largest share while the rest receive their shares according to seniority.

High bride prices have many negative consequences for Jieng and other communities in the Republic of South Sudan. One of the most dangerous social diseases is tribalism, which is virtually destroying the country. One of the best ways of reducing or eliminating tribalism in the long-run is massive inter-tribal marriages . If inter-tribal marriages are practised for twenty years, it will change the fabric of society completely, as aunts, uncles, and grandparents will begin to be shared by children across different tribes. This will likely reduce tribal conflicts.

Currently, even when the wealth required for intermarrying is available, which is difficult in areas without livestock but is becoming easier with the advent of money as a marriage payment, local prejudices prevent intermarriages. However, it's hoped that education will eventually eliminate these barriers. As money becomes increasingly prevalent as the main form of bridal payment, more men from other tribes will be able to afford to marry Jieng girls, whereas currently, members of the Jieng tribe are marrying girls from other tribes, where money payments are accepted over the traditional livestock, cultural items (leopard skin/hide or arrows), or promises of farm labour, is far more common. A time will come when the majority of South Sudanese males will participate in inter-tribal marriages, which will sound a death knell to tribalism in South Sudan and usher in a period of blissfulness.

A moratorium on high bride prices and negative local prejudices may be necessary, as currently, there are some of Jieng communities where prices are so high that many Jieng men cannot afford to marry at all. Sometimes, families give their girls to hard-working men as a long-term investment, knowing that the bridal price will be paid eventually, even if it can't be paid up front.

Men can prove their worth by increasing their agricultural production by ploughing more lands. The resulting increased surplus can be used in a barter system that is highly practised in traditional rural societies. Two big gourds filled with grain—equivalent to around one hundred kilograms each—plus a medium gourd filled with unshelled groundnuts or peanuts—equivalent to twenty-five kilograms—and a small gourd filled with sesame—equivalent to fifteen to twenty kilograms—can be exchanged or bartered for a medium bull. The man will hand over this bull, or a heifer for which he has exchanged it, to his future in-laws. There are rituals and festivals in Jieng communities that require the slaughter of a bull (female cows, especially young ones, are rarely killed for Jieng festivities). By repeating this process over and over again, a poor, hardworking man can provide many bulls and slowly pay the bridal price for his wife.

Alternatively, if a poor man's wife produces a girl as her firstborn, her daughter can get married by the time she is fifteen. When the bridal price is obtained from the daughter's future spouse, her father can use his share to repay his in-laws, who gave him their daughter without payment. The wife's relatives will fix the bridal price, subtracting the number of cows they have received from the their daughter's husband from the sales of agricultural surplus over the years. The husband's relatives will then pay their wei (the number of cows each of a man's relatives pays to their equal on the woman's side of the family in the event of a marriage).

Finally, if neither bartering or using his daughter's bridal price is possible, a man may avoid paying his own bridal price if illness strikes. Illness brings families together, with family members selling cows and goats to contribute financial resources to pay for treatment by traditional healers.

Caring for family members in need is an important part of Jieng culture. If treatment is successful, all family members are happy, and if the sickness results in death, all mourn. The survivors of the deceased, especially children, are taken care of by the rest of the family. In modern times with so much foreign influence, this practice has reduced substantially, and individualism is slowly replacing the traditional sense of community and familial responsibility.

As previously discussed, deceased males are often replaced by their brothers in a practice call ala hot, whereby the brother of a deceased or impotent man marries a woman and produces children on his behalf. This is a very strong and favoured culture, which is practised throughout all Jieng communities, especially those in rural areas.

When females relatives die during their productive years, or when they are barren, without any existing children, their husbands can marry another wife to produce babies for her. If the woman is alive, she can raise and take care of these surrogate babies produced by her husband and the woman who is legally called her wife. If it is not possible for a barren woman's husband to marry a wife for her, the woman's own blood relatives can marry and produce children on her behalf. Women whose children are to be produced for her by a family member must be obedient daughters and wives, and they must follow the norms and dictates of their culture.

Disliked barren women who are unable to find anyone willing to marry them and bear their children often must fend for themselves. For example, there was a famous woman who lived in a village called

Agany in Yirol State, near Makuoragaar village in Western Lakes State. She did not want to have relations with a man, and during the night of consummation following her marriage, she beat her husband and left for town alone. The woman's husband reclaimed his cows, and the woman's relatives abandoned her for refusing her husband. In town, the woman learned how to trade with the local breweries and made a good amount of money, with which she began to buy cows.

Eventually, she accumulated enough cows to afford to marry a girl. She contacted one of her cousins and commissioned him to marry and produce babies for her. The woman's cousin helped her build her own house with enough land around it for her to cultivate crops, and the woman continued to trade in a nearby town, marrying a second wife a couple of years later.

The woman's two wives cooked for her, prepared her bed, boiled water for her bathing, and so on, just like the wives of Jieng men. This dynamic represents a Jieng form of lesbianism.

If they are lucky, as girls become mature, they are married in their early teens or when they reach full maturity at around eighteen years old. Unmarried girls over the age of twenty are referred to as '*nyiir ci buur in*', meaning 'girls who have overstayed their girlhood.' Some of these girls, who often come from bad and unsociable families, may get married eventually, but many go through life without husbands.

Girls are conditioned for a future serving men. They are taught how to make and deliver food, providing separate plates for food (acida and kisra, usually) and gravy, along with clean spoons. Girls must carry trays of food to seated men slowly, and in some Jieng communities, they must kneel while putting the food on the table or on the ground before the men (in old, traditional villages, there are no tables). After delivering the food, girls are to bring a jug of water for the men to drink and wash their mouths with once they have finished eating, then they must return to fetch the empty plates and trays, washing them for their next use.

As girls prepare to become housewives, they learn to respect adults, especially men. Girls are expected to be shy and respectful around men. They are never accompanied when leaving the house to fetch firewood or water or when attending youth dances with female friends. Girls are free to talk with young men, because these conversations are essential for helping these young men to choose their future wives. But if a young man becomes interested in a girl, he is told to let his elders visit hers, so that the two families can become familiar with each other. Girls from outstanding families are readily accepted by their male suitors' elders, but girls who come from undesirable families, such as those with histories of bewitchment, sorcery, or trouble-making, are often shunned by the elders of their prospective suitors, who are told to choose another girl, or for whom a more desirable candidate is chosen. This occurs when the young man is the family member wearing a bead called the *anong yeth jang* or *acieng guen jang*, indicating that he is next in line for marriage.

Boys' marriages are frequently controlled by their elders, because the world of Jieng is one of arranged marriages, but control over girls in this regard is much stronger. Girls have no rights to make major life decisions without the involvement and instruction of their male relatives. They are not allowed to choose their own husbands. When there is not enough food to feed all guests, girls must put aside a small portion of their own food to be consumed by the home's husband when there is nobody else in the house. This practice is called *aguan*, meaning 'something hidden.' Women often have very little to eat. Some men like this arrangement, while others tell their wives to discontinue the practice.

Jieng families train their daughters to obey and submit not because they love them, though an element of love usually exists, but to ensure that their daughter's eventual marriage will not result in divorce and the subsequent refunding of cows. Though divorces do occur in Jieng communities, they are rare and typically only occur as a result of female barrenness, female unfaithfulness, or male impotence with no brother, first cousin, or nephew to takeover procreation duties.

If a man truly loves his wife for her character, her barrenness does not necessarily have to result in divorce. The man can marry a second wife to bear children on his first wife's behalf.

Similarly, unfaithfulness, in most cases, does not result in divorce if the woman has a good character and children. Most Jieng courts, as well as the Jieng community, do not advocate divorce on account of unfaithfulness, because Jieng society is patriarchal, meaning that separations result in children remaining with their fathers. Other co-wives will not take good care of another wife's childen, which is considered detrimental to their development, so the presence of their biological mother is required.

In the absence of close relatives to procreate on behalf of an impotent husband, divorce is often the only option. Cattle are next to God in Jieng mythology, and three of every ten cows paid as bridal prices must be returned, in a practice called arueth, when divorces occur, minus ten cows for each child, a fee called *aruok* in Jieng language.

Jieng society calls it an abomination when all the positive relationships built during a marriage are put asunder by divorce. Divorce has a domino effect, meaning that a single divorce can sometimes result in the destruction of many other marriages. How does this happen? When a divorce happens to one man, he goes to his in-laws to reclaim the balance of his cows. If the in-laws do not have any cows, the man's soon-to-be ex-wife's brothers have to go their in-laws to reclaim the cows they paid as their own bride prices in order to pay back their sister's soon-to-be ex-husband and his family. This forces the divorcing wife's brothers to return their own wives to their families, resulting in unplanned divorces. In Jieng traditional courts, chiefs try their best not to allow divorce unless there is no other option.

Courting is of great cultural importance for young men, because it is part of the process of choosing their future wives.

Abiola, who accepted and loved her culture, respected her elders, who chose a husband for her. Abiola met her suitor for the first time and was asked for her name, her father's name, the name of her father's clan (this was also her clan, as Jieng is a male-dominated society), and the name of her mother's clan.

Boys and girls of the same clan cannot marry each other, as they share the blood of a great, great ancestor and should consider each other siblings, and girls cannot marry maternal male relatives unless they are distanced by three to six generations. In the case of Abiola and her suitor, there was no relation. The young man told Abiola that he wanted her to be his wife, and Abiola told him to let his elders visit hers.

The young man's elders—his father, uncles, brothers, first and second cousins, and some community elders—approved his choice of wife and visited Abiola's elders, by whom they were well received. In order to follow to cultural tradition, Abiola's family had to kill a fat ram or a castrated he-goat or billy. The women then prepared a hearty meal, and the elders were served drinks.

While the women cooked, the men had marriage discussions, generally called *luel e ruai* or *bi ruai luel*. One of Abiola's uncles cleared his throat, called her suitor's father by his nickname or '*rin kek moor*' and asked why the family had visited them. The suitor's father complimented Abiola's family and told the men that they had come to ask for Abiola's hand in marriage to their son.

Abiola's father reacted positively and offered *boog*, meaning 'cow's hide,' to the suitor, his family, and his friends. What does this mean? In the past, in rural areas, Jieng communities used cow hides as mattresses and for seating purposes, as there were no chairs. Offering *boog* meant that the suitor, his family members, and his friends were allowed to visit Abiola, and her other close relatives ,an important step in becoming acquainted and convincing her and other family members of accepting their son as the only man to marry her. In some cases, other suitors may be equally accepted and also granted *boog* by a girl's family. At the end of the acquaintance period, the suitors can compete, and the family will choose the right man for their daughter.

When the guests had eaten and finished their drinks, the suitor's father announced to Abiola's family that they should come to his cattle camp to see his cows in one month.

A month later, the two families met at the suitor's cattle camp. Bulls were swapped for slaughter, and while the women prepared a large meal, the men discussed the bride price—the number of cows that would be given to the Abiola's family as payment for her hand in marriage.

The suitor and his father gave some cows as *hot-ic*, meaning 'inside the chamber or room,' to Abiola's parents, *arop* for her father and *ariek* for her mother.

If there had been other wives (co-wives), they would also have had their share. The number of cows paid as *hot-ic* is dependent on the total number of cows required for the prospective bride price.

Then, *wei* (single: *wai*) costs were shared among Abiola's relatives, according to status and seniority.

Abiola's first suitor offered two hundred cows as bride price for Abiola. Before her family made a decision as to who would be Abiola's husband, they had to consider the offers of her other suitors. Abiola's second suitor offered one hundred and fifty cows, while her third offered two hundred and fifty. Then, Abiola's father called a meeting for all family members, where Abiola's male relatives chose the first suitor as her husband, because he was known to be the hardworking son of a well-respected family, and he liked and respected his in-laws.

Despite offering more cows than any of the other suitors, Abiola's third suitor did not qualify as a good potential husband, because he was known to have bad manners and no respect for his in-laws. Abiola's family knew that he was not the right man for them, but some families would have chosen him, because he had more cows to pay.

Having made their decision, Abiola's family invited the relatives of the first suitor's family to their home to inform them that their son had been chosen to be Abiola's husband. Everybody rejoiced, and Abiola's family received the two hundred cows bride price. Then, a date was fixed for the final marriage ceremony, when Abiola would be given to her husband.

In all ceremonies and decision making, Abiola was absent and was not consulted, and there were no other women present or consulted either.

When Abiola was informed of her family's decision, she accepted it readily. Soon, the time for celebration arrived, and both families danced and rejoiced in Abiola's family's home. Men and women from Abiola's future husband's family sang songs to exalt Abiola's parents' clans and Abiola's close relatives, as well as their own clans and relatives.

While these celebrations were taking place outside, the elderly women of Abiola's family and community, along with her mother, sat with her in the family room and spoke to her about the responsibility of respecting, serving, and caring for her husband and his family. Abiola was reminded not allow her husband or his relatives to say that she was not well-trained as a housewife by her family, and that she was not to entertain the idea of divorce and remarriage unless unavoidable. Abiola's female elders highlighted their own life experiences, teaching Abiola how they had dealt successfully with difficulties. Abiola was told that her husband would test her and that she was to remain calm and focus on passing all intended tests.

After this time with the elderly women of her family, Abiola's mother called her father to prepare their daughter to be given to her new husband. Abiola's father entered and asked his wife to bring the *ghee*. Abiola was smeared with this sweet-smelling oil made from cows' milk, a symbol of high class, in a ceremony called *atoc-toc e nya* or *nya aci jal toc*. Then, the female relatives of Abiola's soon-to-be husband were called to accept her, accompanying her to their home, singing as they went. Some of Abiola's close relatives went with her too. Special women accepted for this role (men are not welcome to partake in this part of the ceremony) are called *dhiop*.

Abiola's family had trained her in all aspects of womanhood, including the values of culture, household management, and housewife duties. The day had now come for her to be given to her husband, who would take over the responsibility of controlling and taking care of her as his wife.

The *dhiop* were put in a big room with their daughter, Abiola, and as soon as they arrived at Abiola's new husband's family's house, a big bull was slaughtered for them, and a big meal was prepared. Cultural norms prevented Abiola's husband from coming close to the house where his wife and in-laws were accommodated. Defying this rule would result in a fine.

If the meat of the first bull was finished, another bull can be slaughtered, or if things were scarce, a big castrated he-goat or ram could have been slaughtered to provide a large meal.

After a Jieng wedding, guests are traditionally supposed to stay for three days before leaving to return to their own homes. During their stay, every measure is taken to make them as comfortable as possible; a lot of food is available throughout the day, and tobacco is provided to smokers; no drinks are provided, because it is culturally a taboo for Jieng women to drink alcohol until they have reached the menopause period.

After three days, Abiola's family left, and Abiola remained with her new married family with two young girls of a similar age, who would help her adjust to her new environment. These girls would do most of the household work until Abiola was initiated into work.

Before the consummation of the new marriage, an important ceremony needed to be conducted by Abiola's husband's father, or in his absence through death, an elderly uncle, preferably a brother of the father.

This ceremony involves the killing of any of a nanny goat, he-goat, (billy), ram, ewe, or wether (castrated male sheep) outside the door of the house where the newlyweds will sleep. The couple is told to jump over the dead animal, enter the house, and close the door after them. This practice is called *thok ala hot* and is supposed to symbolise a prayer to God to give His blessings to the union that is about to begin, that is, allowing the new couple to produce many children and have good health throughout their lives.

Abiola's marriage was now complete, and she was expected to stay with his man for the rest of her life, unless something unusual happened to force her to do otherwise.

Unlike Abiola, Muona was a rebel girl and was against the culture she was born into. Three suitors asked for her hand in marriage, following the same protocols as those who asked for Abiola's. All were given boog to acquaint themselves with Muona and her relatives.

At the end of the *boog* period, the father of Muona's first suitor asked her relatives to come to his cattle camp to see the family's cows. Muona and her suitor's families prepared for wedding discussions, talking about wei and the bride price.

Muona's first suitor's family could afford one hundred and twenty cows. Her second suitor offered one hundred and fifty cows. Her third suitor, whose family was poor in terms of cows, was only able to give fifty cows as bride price. Muona's family members met and chose the first suitor as husband for their daughter. They went to collect the one hundred and twenty cows as bridal payment, and they told the first suitor's family to come for Muona in fifteen days. But Muona was secretly harbouring a different choice.

Muona dearly loved her third suitor, the poor man, and decided to elope with him just five days before her proposed marriage to her family's choice of suitor. The men of Muona's family gathered to fight the third suitor's amily, but Muona's father instead went to the local court, where he spoke with the paramount chief of the area.

The chief dispatched the local police to find Muona and the third suitor, locating and bringing them to court within two days. The paramount chief returned Muona to her family, and her would-be husband was fined a pregnant heifer and warned to leave Muona alone.

The first suitor came to reclaim his cows from Muona's family, because he had found out that Muona did not love him. As punishment for making a choice that had cost her family one hundred and twenty cows, Muona was thoroughly beaten by her brothers, leaving her bedridden for nearly ten days.

After twenty days, Muona escaped again to return to her husband, and together they went into hiding. This time, the young men from both families fought with ebony clubs and other hard tropical plants, aiming to hit each other hard on the head or legs, which can in some cases be fatal.

There were twenty-eight casualties. One of Muona's husband's cousins had his skull terribly broken by one of Muona's brothers, causing bleeding on the brain and leading to his death. One of Muona's cousins had his skull smashed, leaving him with a lifelong disability.

The Government intervened, and all the fighters were taken to court. Muona's brother, who had killed one of her husband's cousins, was given a jail sentence of ten years, while others were given sentences ranging from two to eight years. The family was forced to pay thirty cows as blood compensation. The judge ordered Muona's family to accept her husband's fifty cows as bride price and refrain from further fighting. That is exactly what happened. The family accepted the fifty cows, and Muona remained married to the husband she loved.

When a girl chooses her own husband, it brings a lot of negative consequences. Fights often result in death and serious injuries, and the girl's family can be affected by serious financial repercussions. All of these things create enmity and hostile relationships between families that can last for generations.

For many years, some Jieng girls have fought for the freedom to choose the men they love as their spouses, knowing well the consequences of doing so. To this day, la lute continua, as some Jieng girls continue to reject being forced to marry men they do not love.

In Muona's case, freedom was costly. Muona experienced many strained and damaged relationships with her family for choosing her own husband, and her imprisoned brother never forgave her. Familial relationships like Muona's can be severed forever by cultural rebellion.

There once lived a girl called Anyor (pseudonym) in a neighbouring county of another state bordering the Western Lakes State in the Republic of South Sudan. Anyor was a beautiful girl with many suitors, and her family hoped to get many cows when she got married. But Anyor eloped with a man and disappeared with him to a distant land for nearly thirty years.

Anyor and her husband never had any children, and eventually, tired of severe beatings and general mistreatment from the man she loved, Anyor decided to abandon her marriage and return to her family. When she arrived at her former home, nobody recognised her, and when they finally did, she was beaten by her elder brother, who had inherited their deceased parents' home.

Neighbours warned Anyor's brother not to beat her again for fear of the law. Anyor was in her fifties and could have died from a severe beating, and her brother could have then been hanged.

Heeding this piece of advice, Anyor's brother decided he didn't want anything to do with her and told her to go wherever she liked. A kind neighbour took her in for the night.

The following day, Anyor's other brothers and sisters in nearby villages came, having heard the news of her arrival. A big family meeting took place, and Anyor was told that she was no longer regarded as a member of the family and that she had to find a place in the village where she could build herself a hut or *tukl* to stay in.

Finding an empty place, Anyor built a small hut, where she stayed by herself, cultivating the surrounding land for food. She had few friends. Sometimes, one of her sisters would come to visit her, but none of her brothers ever did.

Anyor remained alone until the day she died. She was buried by some sympathetic distant relations, some neighbours, and just one of her sisters. She was well known in the surrounding villages and became a symbol for teaching girls. Mothers told their daughters, 'Be careful how you behave, or you'll end up like Anyor.'

Not all cases of female disobedience in choosing husbands end so harshly. Some families are kind and can forgive their daughters when they commit such a mistake, reasoning that blood is thicker than water.

But Anyor was not alone in her story. Two centuries before Anyor, there lived Akec Malual of the Padiangbor clan. The totem for the Padiangbor clan is the moon. The people of this clan worship the moon, which they see as one of the ways of reaching God.

Akec was beautiful, but she had strange ideas and behaviour. She was physically very strong and didn't like the idea of sex with men. When she became a woman, she set a condition for her marriage: any suitor interested in asking her hand for marriage had to wrestle with her first. If she knocked him down, he was disqualified, and if he knocked her down, she would marry him.

Over the years, many suitors came to challenge Akec, and none of them succeeded in knocking her down. Akec's relatives realised that no man would succeed in knocking her down, and that the chances of her being married were very slim.

The family decided to chase Akec away from the house. Akec found a nice location, where she built her own house, cultivated her own food, and stayed alone for the rest of her life. She became well known throughout the land as a legend.

Jieng woman like Muona, Anyor, and Akec have always fought for their right to choose their own husbands with little success. But the introduction of education by the British Colonial Administration and its allies, especially the Catholic and the Anglican Protestant Churches (Episcopal Church), which operated under the umbrella of the Colonial Government, brought positive results.

Towards the end of the nineteenth century, Christian missionaries in South Sudan started opening bush, elementary, and intermediate schools. Only boys were eligible to attend. In Jieng territories, it was difficult to find a sufficient number of boys in any given area to start school, as parents were reluctant to send their sons to foreign institutions whose programs they didn't know or understand. It was completely out of the question to send girls to school at that time.

The local colonial administrators asked the chiefs, the leaders of the people, to send their sons to schools first in the hopes that others would follow. At first, only a few pupils attended schools, but over the years, the number of students increased substantially.

Those who started school between 1900 and 1910 finished elementary and intermediate schooling, and because there were no further schools to go to, they had to look for gainful employment. Getting employed as teachers in mission schools and as clerks, police officers, and prison wardens in the colonial system gave them important status in their local communities, because colonial administration employees wielded considerable authority.

The meagre salaries of these new graduates endeared them to their people, as they were the first educated class. This earliest money had big value. The pound was divided into piasters (one hundred piasters to a pound—for between ten and thirty piasters, one could buy a heifer or bull), *tarifa* (equal to half a piaster, enough to buy half a kilo of meat or a basin of grain), and *malim* (one hundred *malims* to a piaster, enough buy a box of matches or a single cigarette). These coins were usually made of silver, copper, and other metallic alloys, such as brass. Then came the pound.

Early salary earners were able to buy cows and goats and modern items. Goats, sheep, and cows remained the most valuable assets to the local people, and any townsperson who bought them for the people of their village became instantly famous and important in the eyes of locals.

Many native people started sending their sons to schools in the hope that they would buy them more cows when they finished schooling, and this idea became the biggest promoter of education in Jieng territories. By the 1950s, the number of children going to schools had multiplied by thousands compared to 1900.

Increasing rates of education among natives caused a whole new social class to form: the intelligentsia, the educated class. This group of people thought and behaved differently to the local natives. Their contact with new ideas from foreign culture through education gave them a positive attitude towards girls and women. They realised that educating girls was not only beneficial to the girl herself, her family, and her husband, but also to society at large, so they began to send their daughters to school with their sons.

There are some great examples of this shift. There was once a girl whose father was a villager, but her paternal uncle, her father's younger brother, who was educated and worked in town, came to take her to town to look after his young children. Because the girl's uncle valued female education, he let his niece attend school with his children. The girl outperformed her cousins academically, which made her uncle very happy.

When the girl's father discovered that his brother had allowed his daughter to attend school, he boiled with anger, believing that education spoiled girls and their ability to earn good bride prices. He decided to fight his brother and take his daughter back to his village. He took his spears and headed for the town, where he went straight to the police station, where his brother worked as a police officer. On arrival, the girl's father launched a succession of spears at his brother, all missing their target, before the policemen realised the attack and began to shoot bullets from their guns, forcing him to drop his weapons.

The girl's father was arrested and charged with assaulting police personnel and a government institution. He was locked up overnight, then taken to the judge, who sentenced him to three months' imprisonment, a light sentence because nobody had been hurt in the attack.

The girl's uncle requested that her father was brought to him before his release at the end of his sentence. The uncle returned the father's spears and told him, 'You have now been released. If you remain in town for two more hours, you will be arrested and imprisoned again. If you return from the village with the same intention, you will be arrested and given more years in prison. Your daughter will never go back to the village, because she is now being educated.' The girl's father left immediately for the village, never to return. He decided to forget his daughter, considering her dead.

Three years on, the girl's uncle developed a serious illness and soon died. During this time, South Sudan was in serious crisis, struggling to withstand political upheaval that was crippling the country.

After burying her husband, the girl's aunt and the rest of the family, including the girl, went to stay in Kakuma refugee camp in Kenya as a refugee family. The girl's uncle's wife applied for asylum in the United States of America, and after two years, her application was successful. The whole family moved to the United States, where the children resumed their schooling. The girl excelled in her studies and eventually entered medical school. She graduated successfully and became employed.

The girl's cousins also graduated from college and found work, repositioning their once poor family as financially successful. The girl met a well-off young man from her own area of South Sudan, who had also emigrated to the United States. They eventually got married.

Thinking of her estranged family in South Sudan, the girl began to make contact with people from home and was lucky to connect with one of her cousins, who told her that her father had run into serious misfortune. Most of his wives were dead, including the girl's mother; he'd lost nearly all of his cattle wealth; some of his sons were alive but destitute; and he had gone blind and was being looked after by a surviving middle-aged wife.

The girl and her husband decided to help her family in any way they could. They rented comfortable accommodation in Kampala and employed housemaids, then they airlifted the girl's father and his wife to Kampala. They hired an eye specialist to perform an eye operation to restore the girl's father's sight. After six months, his health had improved drastically.

When the girl's father had recovered, she and her husband visited him in Uganda. The girl's father was deeply happy to see his daughter, whom he'd assumed dead. For the first time, he mourned for the untimely death of his late brother and thanked and praised him for putting his daughter through school.

The girl's father thanked her aunt and asked her for forgiveness for having attempted to kill his brother. He blamed himself for having been a fool.

Before returning to the United States, the girl and her husband gave her father enough money to buy one hundred cows for himself and a further one hundred and fifty as bride price for their marriage. They bought clothes both for the relatives who remained in the village, along with mattresses, beds, bedsheets, and a mobile for the girl's father, which he could use to contact them when in need. Finally, the girl's family members were airlifted back to their village in South Sudan.

The other villagers were surprised to see the girl's father in such good health, restored eyesight and with so much money and so many modern items from Kampala. He told them that he had gotten these things from the daughter his brother had sent to school.

The message of the benefits of girls' education spread quickly throughout the territory and beyond. The girl's father became an advocate of female education, and negative attitudes towards girls' education in the area began to be reversed, with many local parents allowing their daughters to attend schools.

In another example, a second girl escaped political upheaval in South Sudan. Her father was a primary school teacher, and he and the rest of the family failed to understand what this girl did.

The boys escaped to fight against the oppressive government, but the girl was more interested in furthering her education without disturbance. In Sudan, once a girl is matured, any young man can come to ask for her hand in marriage, and in most cases, she is expected to accept. Instead of giving up her education to get married, the girl left for the United States, where she studied a bachelor's degree in accounting, attended various accounting institutes, and became a highly qualified accountant, securing a well-paying job with a big company.

Soon, the girl met a man from her own area in South Sudan, who also had a well-paying job. She explained to her fiancé that her father and the rest of her family were angry with her for having escaped Sudan without their knowledge and that she needed to make amends before they could get married.

The girl flew back to Sudan alone, leaving her fiancé in the United States. She located her paternal uncle and explained everything, asking him to intervene and convince her parents to forgive her and accept her back as their daughter. The uncle agreed to be the peacemaker and approached the family to explain everything. The girl's parents were eager to forgive their daughter. Her mother accompanied her uncle to the hotel she was staying at and brought her home.

The family threw a big party to welcome their daughter home. The girl's father told the gathering family members and friends that his daughter was completely forgiven, especially as she'd returned highly educated and unmarried.

The girl checked with local real estate and purchased a seven-room mansion surrounded by a big wall. She furnished the house and bought two cars: one for her father and another for her mother. She hired guards to protect the home.

After spending several days at her parents' house, the girl asked her mother and father to take a walk with her to one of the suburbs of the city. Here, she welcomed them to the mansion, showing them all the rooms, then leading them to the family room, where the keys and papers for the property sat on a table. The girl gave the house to her father, and her mother began to weep with joy.

Outside the house, two cars were parked, and the girl gave the keys for these, too, to her parents. Her father collapsed with happiness. A few hours later, the girl and her parents surprised the rest of the family with the news, and within three days, the family had moved into their new home.

The father threw a big party, where he slaughtered a bull and some rams, and there was plenty of food and drink. The girl's father delivered a wonderful speech, praising female education.

Two weeks later, the girl called her fiancé in the United States, asking him to come to Sudan for their wedding now that she had made peace with her family. Within three days, he'd arrived. First, he went to his family, told them of his intentions, and asked his father and uncles to visit the girl's family to ask for a boog and the hand of the girl as his wife.

The man's elders came to visit the girl's family and were well received. Everything was agreed upon, and the courting period was set to last a month. Then, the relatives of the two families met to discuss the bride price. The man's relatives gave thirty cows—in an area where bride prices were usually below fifty cows—to the girl's family, which they accepted readily. Within a week, wedding celebrations were conducted; the two families were joined.

A few weeks later, the happy newlyweds flew back to the United States, their second home, to continue with their careers and start a family of their own. Before leaving, the young man gave a lot of money to his new wife's family to fund children's education and other family concerns.

Increasingly, anecdotes from people living in Jieng territory have begun to send a clear message about the value of female education for girls, their families, the families into which they marry, and society as a whole.

Most Jieng families, both urban and rural, have accepted education for girls. Female enrolment in schools has increased dramatically, but the number of girls sitting secondary entrance examinations (Primary 8 leaving examinations) remains less than a third of the number of girls who start in Primary 1.

Once the girls reach the age of fifteen, many of them, whether in school or not, get married, mostly against their will, and others become pregnant. A very small percentage of them, around twenty percent, like Muona, take freedom in choosing their own partners.

In Jieng communities, girls are perceived as sources of wealth. The cows they are married with are used to fund their brothers' marriages and to sustain their families. Despite positive changes of attitude towards girls' education, pockets of resistance remain intact.

In Rumbek Civil Hospital, I met a girl whose hopes of education were cruelly dashed. She was the only girl in a family with three brothers. She had just passed her secondary entrance examinations with flying colours and was hoping to attend Rumbek Senior Secondary School.

The young girl emerged from the hospital's patients' ward crying. I asked her what was wrong. She said that her elder brother had just lost his legs in a gun fight. Her family had decided to find a wife for her brother as soon as he was well enough, so he could produce children for himself as soon as possible. To acquire the necessary cows for her brother's fiancée, this girl would be married to a very rich man, who had come to ask for her hand. This meant that her education was over, despite the fact that she'd been accepted to Rumbek Senior Secondary School.

I could do nothing for the girl, but I thought of her. Two days later, one of my relatives became seriously ill and was admitted to the ward where the girl's brother was staying. I visited, carrying local tobacco, which I split between my relative and the girl's brother.

Within three months, the girl's brother's wounds had healed, and he was discharged from the hospital. His sister had gotten married to a villager and had earned a bride price of one hundred and fifty cows for the family.

The girl's brother was married for a price of sixty cows, leaving the remaining cows for her other two brothers.

The girl was like a sacrificial lamb for her brothers. She will remain married to her villager husband for the rest of her life, so that her brothers may remain with their wives for all of their lives.

There are often debates about exorbitant bride prices. Cows earned from a daughter's marriage are used for her brothers' wives and for family sustenance. Some cultures have misconceptions about Jieng marriages, saying that Jieng traditions are about selling girls. This is untrue. Bride prices pay for a girl's reproductive organs, which produce babies for her husband, and for her services. This is clear, because when a woman is found to be barren, most husbands divorce them immediately or seek an additional wife.

Sometimes, nature acts in strange ways, giving five boys and just one girl to a family, while giving five girls and just one boy to another. A single boy with the five sisters is called juol in Jieng language and is likely to be very rich, benefitting from the bride prices of all of his sisters. On the other hand, a single girl with five brothers is likely to struggle to earn a bride price high enough to accommodate the marriages of each of her brothers. These girls pray, and sometimes lie, to acquire enough cows.

For example, in the Western Lakes State in the Republic of South Sudan, there lived a great paramount chief who had many wives, marrying a new wife each year and giving them to his sons for reproductive purposes.

In his state, there lived a girl with five brothers. She had been thinking about how she would help her brothers afford the bride prices for their wives. One day, the girl was impregnated by a local boy. Her brothers wanted to kill her, because her pregnancy meant that she would no longer fetch many cows for her marriage, certainly not enough for all of them.

The girl's father begged her brothers not to kill her, because she had promised to name the man who had impregnated her in the court, and he may have had the cows the family needed.

The girl went with her father and brothers to the court, where she was put in front of the chiefs and asked to name the man who'd impregnated her. 'Angelbook,' she addressed the paramount chief, 'have you forgotten the day you called me into your room, two months ago? A month after that date, I missed my period.'

The chief said, 'Please, repeat what you have just said loud and clear for everybody to hear.'

Before the girl could repeat herself, the court exploded into laughter, because everyone had already heard. When the laughter died down, and the chief called his eldest son and the girl's father and brothers to come forward. 'Take this old man and his sons to the cattle camp and give them one hundred cows until a proper marriage can be conducted,' the chief told his eldest son. He knew the girl had lied, but as far as he was concerned, it was a good lie, because it reminded people of his virility.

The chief sent his guard to call his eldest wife, and when she arrived, he instructed her to take the girl, his new wife, and to look after her until he came home in the evening.

Seven months later, the girl delivered her child, a proper marriage was conducted, and a further eighty cows were added to the previous one hundred, finalising the marriage. All of the girl's brothers got married, and there was even a balance of cows left to sustain the family.

Women are at the centre of life in Jieng culture. They are trained and conditioned extensively, making many women think they are not being mistreated. Traditional people believe that female training is for the betterment of women and society. Only rebel women see that women are cruelly mistreated and denied their human rights.

Jieng girls are not alone in being trained. Boys, too, are trained from an early age, and their training is almost opposite to that of girls. In Jieng culture, a man's world is very different from that of a woman. Man's world is seen as difficult and hard, so training for boys is also difficult, designed to teach courage and endurance.

Boys are trained in fishing, hunting, cultivating food crops, and maintaining livestock, especially cattle. Looking after cattle is particularly gruelling, because there are times when men must fight an attacking lion or a thieving cattle rustler to protect the cattle. Shying away is considered an act of cowardice, the worst accusation a Jieng man can face.

Young boys are taught to endure hunger, because in undeveloped parts of Jieng territory, there are often periods when food is hard to come by.

In most Jieng communities, when boys are initiated into manhood, there are certain rituals that they must endure without showing fear. For example, in the Agaar community, the initiation of boys into manhood involves a ceremony in which a number of lines (usually between six and eight lines) are inserted into the forehead with a sharp knife, while the boy sits cross-legged and straight. The man inserting the lines stands in front of the boy, catches his head ,inserts the sharp knife on the lower left side of the head and slowly turning his head from one side to the other, tearing the skin with the knife. The boy is not to show any sign of fear and must remain calm until all the lines are put across his forehead. Then, he bends his head down so that the blood flows into a hole dug in front of him. As the wounds heal, for four to six weeks, the initiated boys move together through the houses of each of their parents. In Jieng language, this practice is called gar e nhom. If a boy shows fear, he is labelled a coward, bringing such shame to himself and his family that most of these boys leave the community. In some Jieng communities, girls also participate in similar initiations into womanhood.

Boys are also trained to be proud and to avoid doing bad things. They are taught to be men of dignity and integrity. In Jieng society, everybody is equal, and Jieng people have a saying to express this concept: '*Aril agut ci ran hone tol*,' meaning 'Everybody is the same, even the man living in the smallest hut/tukl.' Jieng people do not have kings, because they wouldn't like anybody to appear excessively more important than the rest of the community. Jieng tend to be democratic, allowing leaders to serve their communities for a time, then allowing somebody new to take over.

CHAPTER FOUR

The Reproductive Period, the Family Formation Years

Marriage is one of the oldest human institutions and is practised in human societies all around the world. It is one of the institutions that distinguishes man from other animals.

When two young people get married, they begin to form a separate family. Most world religions sanction this type of union. In some cultures, including Western culture, love is considered a necessary, or at least preferred, condition for marriage. In other cultures, most commonly those prevalent in economically underdeveloped countries, marriages can acceptably occur without love, in accordance with the interests of relatives.

The man who married Abiola was not in love with her, but Abiola's family thought he was a decent man, who would take good care of their daughter. When Abiola got married, her family relinquished their control of her to her husband, who was to be responsible for her for the rest of her life. Love came later, cultivated by time together. Abiola's first duty was to her husband. She had to make sure that he was well-fed, cooking for him at least twice a day if food resources were available.

According to Jieng culture, a wife is also responsible for taking care of all other relatives, especially parents (who often move in when in need of care in their old age), brothers, and sisters, when they come to visit.

Every morning, a wife gets up, cleans the compound, and fetches water for the day if there is none in the house. In rural areas, water sources are often far away. Women have to walk to the sources, collect water, and carry it back on their heads using jerry cans and huge earthen pots.

Cooking is a woman's domain and is a difficult undertaking. Grain must be pounded traditionally using mortar and pestle to produce a fine flour for making acida. Nowadays, there are grinding mills in rural areas that produce fine flour quickly and easily, but they are few and scattered in the villages, meaning that women have to walk long distances to reach them and then wait in long queues. Sometimes, women go to nearby towns to have their grain ground into fine flour, taking enough to make flour for at least two weeks.

Women also have to fetch firewood and vegetables from the forests on a daily basis, and they have to handwash all dishes, plates, and cutlery, as well as clothes and bedsheets. If there are no other females in the house to help her, a wife has to do all this work by herself. Fortunately, extended family relationships, especially females, are usually available to help the wife in her normal household chores.

The main reason that young Jieng people get married is to produce children, who will continue the family line. In Jieng culture, women are expected to produce children until they reach menopause. But Jieng women breastfeed their children for two and a half years before weaning. During this period, and for six months following it, parents do not engage in any sexual activity, because it is believed that this can make the breastfeeding child sick. This tradition is called thek e thiang or and is to be respected at all costs. This time it allows a woman to regain her health ahead of her next pregnancy.

In Jieng tradition, siblings' births are usually around three years apart, and this reduces the number of children born during a woman's reproductive years, thus serving as an indirect form of family planning. The tradition has undergone some changes as a result of influences from foreign cultures, but it is still practised in rural areas, which are less influenced by foreign ideas.

There are many cultural taboos for married Jieng women. They are free to travel without any suspicion from any member of the family, but they must not have any serious conversations men who are unknown to the family, or they may be suspected of having an affair. Gossip spreads quickly, and unfaithfulness is severely punishable.

If caught red-handed, an unfaithful woman's lover may be beaten by her husband or one of his male relatives, sometimes to death. If the woman's husband kills her lover, he may face long-term imprisonment or hanging, but this is unlikely if the act was committed in his house, as the law may consider him to have been provoked beyond reasonable doubt. Alternatively, the woman's lover may kill her husband in self defence, leading to serious legal repercussions.

If no death occurs, an adulterer is taken to the traditional court and accused of having an affair with somebody's wife. The usual punishment for such a crime is a payment of seven cows to the husband of the unfaithful wife. This is called akor.

If a woman is not unfaithful but is a victim of rape, the punishment for her rapist remains the akor payment, but her husband will not blame her or accuse her of being unfaithful.

After an akor payment has been settled, an unfaithful woman is asked by the traditional court which of her two husbands or lovers she prefers, the old or the new. If the woman has children with her old husband and chooses to return to him, he is expected to forgive his wife and take her back. Occasionally, a former husband refuses to accept his wife, and a divorce takes place, with the husband getting back some of his bride price in cows, depending on how many children he and his wife have.

There are two circumstances in which divorce is immediate: if the woman chooses her new lover, or if she has no children with her husband.

If divorce takes place, it must be complete, so that the woman is free. This means that all the cows that were paid by the husband and his family as bride price must be rebalanced in a practice called *arueth*, whereby three cows for every ten cows paid as bride price are returned to the person who paid the wai. For each child the couple has, the husband has to pay ten cows, a payment called *aruok*, (singular) or *arok* (plural). This is a legal divorce, and the woman is free to remarry, which is important, because an incomplete or illegal divorce could lead any children the woman shares with a future husband to be considered as being born out of wedlock, meaning that they would belong to the improperly divorced legal husband.

In the northern part of the Western Lakes State, there lived a couple who were happily married and had three children. All of a sudden, the woman, Lady Aneet (pseudonym) was struck by leprosy, a dreaded infectious disease that affects Jieng communities. Her husband was horrified and took his eldest child away from her, then sending her away to her relatives with her two youngest children. Lady Aneet's brother took no pity on her and chased her away from his house. She then headed for Rumbek City, where she became a beggar for daily food and suffered greatly.

One day, Lady Aneet made a fateful decision. She decided to go into the deep forest and allow wild animals to end the lives of she and her children. As she headed towards the forest, rain began to fall heavily, and she hurried to shelter in a roadside house.

There was nobody in the empty kitchen, as homeowners were

inside their house. The downpour continued for several hours, and the children got cold and hungry and began to cry.

The homeowners heard the cries, and when the rain stopped, the family's son, a military officer who had just arrived home from business in Kampala, came to investigate.

The man, called Rualmaker (pseudonym) was compassionate and invited Lady Aneet to sit with him in a rakuba, a kind of parasol built in most South Sudanese homes to provide shade. He ordered his sisters to prepare food for Lady Aneet and her children.

Rualmaker asked Lady Aneet who she was and why she was in such a horrible state, and she explained her hardships to him. When the food was ready, Rualmaker's sisters brought it out, and Lady Aneet and the elder of the two children ate hungrily, the other child too young to eat solids and very weak and malnourished, having been being breastfeed by such a hungry mother.

Rualmaker realised that Lady Aneet was all alone in the world without anyone to care about her. He decided to let her stay in the house for a while. At the end of his holidays, he took her to Kampala, where he rented her an apartment and took her to the hospital, where she started treatment for her leprosy and her children were checked for disease.

Two years later, Lady Aneet was cured and beautiful. She thought about how to repay Rualmaker for all he had done for her and for her children, and she eventually decided to give herself to him as a wife. She'd been rejected by her husband and relatives and thought that she was free to do what she liked.

Lady Aneet sought audience with Rualmaker and said, 'Rualmaker, what you have done for me and my children is so glorious and unforgettable, I have no human words to express my gratitude. I have thought about what I can do to repay you for your kindness, and I have decided to give myself to you as a wife. Should you want to marry more wives in the future, you are completely free to do so.'

Rualmaker was stunned and felt very touched. 'Aneet,' he said, 'I didn't help you for marriage or payment. I had sympathy for you, because you were alone in the world.'

'It is because I am all alone in the world that I need you to be my husband,' said Aneet. 'Then, I wouldn't be alone anymore.'

Rualmaker and Aneet discussed this topic for a month, until Rualmaker, at long last, accepted Aneet as his wife. They produced three children to accompany the two from Aneet's previous marriage, and they decided to return to South Sudan, where Rualmaker was planning to go and see Aneet's family and marry her legally.

When they reached Rumbek City, Aneet met the brother who had chased her away. He was very friendly and glad to find his sister healthy with five children, pregnant with a sixth, and her new husband.

Rualmaker and Aneet went to stay with Rualmaker's relatives in his father's house, and Aneet's brother came to visit several times.

Rualmaker informed his would-be brother-in-law that he was planning to speak with the family about legally marrying Aneet. One day, Aneet's brother came and told Rualmaker's relatives that he would like to take his sister's children to a nearby house, where they would be seen by his family members. Instead, he took them on a bus to Maper, his home village, seventy miles north of Rumbek City. He delivered the children to Aneet's former husband and told him that Aneet was now pregnant to another man.

Aneet's first husband immediately filed a lawsuit against Rualmaker for taking his wife illegally. He came to Rumbek City to attend the traditional court with Rualmaker and Aneet, where Rualmaker was ordered to pay seven cows as akor. The traditional law was enforced. Rualmaker and Aneet's three children, as well as their unborn child, were considered to be born out of wedlock, making them the legal children of Anneet's first husband, who she had not divorced. Aneet's first husband reclaimed his wife, and though Aneet tried to explain that she had been chased away and abandoned by her husband and her relatives, the court did not find her defence legitimate.

Rualmaker filed an appeal to the Court of Appeals (the High Court of the land) for his children and Aneet, who refused to go back to her former husband. He also encouraged Aneet to file for divorce through the Court of Appeals. This modern court, based on English laws and modern norms, may help Rualmaker and Aneet to win their case, reversing the rulings of the traditional court.

The prevailing cultural philosophy among Jieng people is that it is important to produce as many children as possible. Having many children is considered a blessing from the Gods and ancestors. Some girls start having babies when they're just thirteen years old. These women sometimes produce twelve or thirteen children before becoming menopausal.

It's considered important for women in most third world countries to have many children, because child mortality rates are very high as a result of tropical diseases and underdeveloped medical facilities. Often in third wold countries, only six or seven of a woman's thirteen children will survive childhood.

In most Jieng communities, especially those in in rural areas, women nearing menopause encourage their husbands to look for younger wives. Some men marry as many as twenty wives. Usually, the last wife is called ting adeet, meaning 'the last wife.' The ting adeet is expected to take care of her husband in his old age. This idea of having a number of wives releases elderly women from the responsibility of taking care of their husbands, thus giving them a sense of rest for the first time in their marriages.

Elderly Jieng women are responsible for the care of their grandchildren. When children are weaned and taken to cattle camps, they often stay there with their grandmothers, who drink milk with them and occasionally get village food items such as peanut and sesame paste, beans, fine grain flour, and green grams from the mothers of the children.

Reaching this stage of life is something most women look forward to, because it is a period of rest and freedom. At this age, women are revered and are freer than ever before to do as they please, smoke tobacco, and drink small amounts of alcohol.

The division of labour between the sexes in Jieng communities is very complex. According to Jieng tradition, all activities requiring strenuous physical effort, such as fighting wars, looking after cattle, building houses, and cultivating food crops are the responsibilities of men. Women are assigned less strenuous activities, as they are considered to be physically weaker. Women are tasked with cutting grass to be used for roofing houses, making earthenware utensils, thatching roofs, milking cows, cleaning compounds, and smearing and plastering hut walls.

Some cooking-related tasks are physically difficult, but in primitive times, they were assigned to women, because people did not wear clothing, and it was feared that men's sexual organs, called cul or chul and nhian in Jieng language ('penis' and 'testicles'), would catch fire, jeopardising procreation and the continuation of the Jieng race. Today, Jieng men still have nothing to do with cooking; most men never even enter the kitchen.

When Jieng people grow old, women usually stay with one of their daughters, while men stay with one of their sons. When a woman has no daughters, she may stay with one of her sons, but this arrangement is fraught with conflict. Old mothers and young wives often argue about their ability to care for their son and husband.

CHAPTER FIVE

The Role of a Woman and a Man in Jieng Society

A Jieng woman has three main functions or roles in her community: bringing wealth to her people, delivering services to those staying with her, and producing children for her husband.

When a Jieng man gets married, he has to pay some form of bride price, usually paid in cows. This bride price can vary between thirty and four hundred cows, depending on wealth and community context. When a girl is born into any Jieng family, she is dearly welcomed, because her family knows that she will one day marry and bring wealth.

As the girl-child grows up, she is regularly reminded that she will bring a lot of cattle wealth to her immediate family, providing enough cows to enable her brothers to pay bride prices for their wives, with remaining cattle given to her extended family members and used for the upkeep of the family.

This idea is greatly emphasised, so that the girl understands that she must be married with a good number of cows as bride price in order to serve her family and prove that she loves them.

In Jieng culture, cows are the most important animals on earth, because milk is instant food, and all the other parts of the cow—meat, hide, horns, hooves—can be used.

It is considered the cultural right of a girl's relatives to benefit from her marriage. When a girl is married in a Jieng community, all her immediate and extended family members are welcomed to share and enjoy the wealth she has brought, and in some cases, clan members are also included in this tradition. This means that Jieng women are essential to building bonds between different peoples and cementing these relationships in a way that brings peaceful coexistence between different clans.

In Jieng culture, a woman is not only a symbol of wealth; she is a symbol of peace though the relationships that her marriage creates.

From the time a girl is five or six years old, her mother teaches her to perform simple household tasks, and by the time she is seven or eight, she can sweep the compound, wash dishes, and perform other, more substantial tasks.

As a girl grows up, her household duties increase accordingly, and by the time she reaches puberty at around twelve or thirteen years of age, she is ready for her mother to pass on most housekeeping responsibilities.

Household activities are repetitive and must be performed on a daily basis. They include general house cleaning, fetching water and firewood, buying charcoal, washing clothes, cooking, pounding grain into fine flour or taking it to the grinding mills, washing children, boiling bathing water for the men of the house, and caring for guests. Women must complete these chores without any complaints, because these chores are considered a woman's duty.

The purpose of marriage is to produce children that will continue the family line and the human race. Because Jieng society is patriarchal, all children bear their father's name, family, and clan, which is why girls' relatives are paid a bride price when she marries.

Children are highly welcomed, appreciated, and loved, and they are raised to believe that they belong to their paternal families. If children cannot come from a marital union, a series of scenarios can take place.

If a husband is infertile, his wife is given to one of his brothers, who can produce children on his behalf. This is called alahot, meaning 'entering the house of a brother.' Children born of these circumstances bear the name and are culturally considered the offspring of their impotent father, dead or alive, though their biological father is their paternal uncle. The children's uncle will deny any attributions of their parentage, because it is considered an abomination for a virile brother to call his dead or impotent brother's children his own.

If the source of infertility is a woman, her husband's family can marry another wife to their son. If the woman is still young and is not well-liked by her husband and his relatives, she can divorce her husband and return to her family, where she can be remarried if a suitor is interested in her. Such women are called ayol yom, aderjook, or adejook. There are known cases where such women have remarried and produced healthy babies with other men.

If a woman is remarried to a series of men and cannot produce any babies, she is returned to her family, and sometimes her brother can marry a wife on her behalf, producing children who will bear the name of his barren sister. When this happens, the woman becomes like another son to her family.

In some cases, barren women do not divorce their husbands, staying married for love.

In one Jieng community, there was once a couple who really loved each other and got married when the woman was around fifteen years old. They tried to have children for a couple of years, and when they failed to realise this dream, they went to the hospital for a check-up.

The doctor told the couple that there was nothing biologically wrong with either of them and that they would probably produce children soon. After another fifteen of marriage, there were still no children. The woman decided that her husband would have to marry another woman, but he refused, saying that the presence of another woman might create tension and destroy the prevailing peace and love in their marriage.

The woman insisted, involving her husband's elderly male relatives, who tried to convince him of the importance of having his own children. Eventually, the husband agreed to take another wife.

When the young wife arrived, the husband called for a family meeting. The older wife told the young one that she did not consider her a co-wife but a daughter. She intended to act as a grandmother to the children the young woman would bring forth. The young wife agreed. The husband decreed that these words must be kept as promises and warned his young wife sternly that she must not consider the first wife as a co-wife, only as a mother. He warned both women that if they broke their promises, they would face his wrath.

The young wife fell pregnant quickly and produced her first son. Three years later, she fell pregnant again and delivered a baby girl. The old wife was very happy and excited by these arrivals. She took good care of the first-born boy and would soon also care for the newborn girl. The family was very happy.

One day, the old wife missed her period, and she thought she must be sick. She asked her husband to accompany her to the hospital, where they were both shocked to be told that the old wife was pregnant at last. All who knew the family were very happy.

The husband and the old wife decided to lessen the lactation period, weaning their children after six months, allowing the woman to fall pregnant again. At the end of her reproductive period, the old wife had seven children and the young wife had ten.

What if the old wife had been barren forever? What would have happened? The husband would have married another woman for her, who would have produced babies for her. If the husband was too old to produce offspring, he would have asked one of his cousins to do this on his behalf, and the children would still have borne the name of his wife.

Looking at the role of a man in any Jieng community is like looking at a role of a king in a kingdom. Men are at the heads of their families. Everything carries their name—wives, property, children—and they control their wives, children, wealth, and so on. No part of family life happens without a man's approval.

Men are defenders of territory, protecting their domain when invaders attempt to take over or loot. Men also look after cattle when they are released to graze far away from the cattle camps. To Jieng people, cattle are the most important asset, so this is a highly valued duty. Looking after released cattle is one of the most difficult tasks in any Jieng community. The cows must be protected, because they can be attacked by lions. Many young men have been killed by lions while defending their grazing cattle. Young men who kill lions to protect cattle are instantly respected by their communities and are called courageous, intrepid, and men of integrity.

Men are expected to be talented farmers, cultivating crops of nuts, grains and millets, beans, and more for their families. When a man's children are young, his wife or wives help him to carry out this difficult job. However, as his sons grow up, they begin to relieve him from this work. When a man has several wives, the sons of each take over the responsibility of farming with help from their mothers and sibling. Their father moves from house to house, checking that all is going well.

If a man is well-off in terms of cattle, he often spends much of his time staying in a cattle camp, where he drinks milk and occasionally enjoys fish, wild meat, and hot acida mixed with ghee. For Jieng people, this is the ultimate high life. Milk is thought to repair all bodily damages, acting as a detoxing agent and improving health. In cattle-camps, Jieng men of seventy years and older are healthy and strong.

Men are also responsible for providing rare food items, such as wild meat and fish, for their families. During the dry season, from January to March, most men take their families to the toic area, where there are many rivers full of fish. They stay in their cattle camps and bring back fresh fish, some of which is eaten fresh, while the rest is prepared for drying. Over the three-month dry season, this dried fish accumulates into big bundles.

Hunting wild animals like buffaloes and antelopes is common in Jieng territories and is a popular sport enjoyed by most males, especially the youth. A lot of dry meat is acquired during the dry season. By the end of March, most men and their families return to their villages laden with bundles of dry fish and wild meat, ready to prepare their farms for the coming rainy season.

During farming, families eat well, consuming an abundance of fresh vegetables. Leaves of many vegetables, like okra and malokia, are boiled and served with dried fish or meat mixed with little bit of peanut butter that form a kind of gravy or thick soup called combo, to be eaten with acida or kisra. This is a favourite dish among Jieng people.

Many people wonder why meat was such a rare commodity in traditional Jieng societies, particularly as cows, goats, and sheep are so much more prevalent than in any other tribe in the Republic of South Sudan. But in Jieng culture, it is taboo to kill an animal for meat only. Animals are only killed when celebrations such as marriages, religious rites, sickness rituals, and fattening traditions demand animal sacrifices.

Traditionally, Jieng people did not believe that diseases were caused by viruses or bacteria, instead blaming sickness on angry Gods or ancestors, who demanded to be appeased. There is a group of people collectively called *tit* (single: *tiet*) who represent the medical profession. These people specialise in identifying the angry Gods or ancestors who might have caused a sickness. They search for a reason for the affliction and decide what should be done to make the sick person well again.

When sickness strikes, families invite a *tiet* to come and perform *tiit*, (an examination) investigating the disease, its causes, and its solutions.

The tiet asks for a calabash full of water, which he throws grasses into. Sometimes, these grasses lie flat on the water in the calabash, while other times, they stand perpendicular.

The tiet looks intently into the water in the calabash. After a while, he clears his throat, and begins to tell the family his findings. He might say that an ancient ancestor has been forgotten by his grandchildren to the extent that nobody sacrificed a bull on his grave, or he might say that a given God is angry because some of the family's girls are married and no cow or bull has been given.

With this knowledge, the family kills a cow or bull to appease the concerned God or ancestor or provides a cow of a certain colour to the God or ancestor to be kept as their property. The *tiet* is usually given a female goat or sheep as payment for his services.

One common tradition for Jieng youth is to go for fattening. Groups of fifteen to twenty-five youths, girls and boys, gather a good number of milking cows and some bulls to be slaughtered for meat. The girls cook and milk the cows, while the boys take care of the cows and help with milking. For six weeks, the youths eat excessively, drinking a lot of daily milk and slaughtering a new bull every three to five days. Some of the meat is roasted, while the rest is simply boiled to be eaten and its thick, fatty soup drunk. A good quantity of *ghee* is put into hot acida and eaten with spoons made from cows' horns and ebony.

To provide shade and shelter from the rain, the youths build a long grass-roofed structure on poles called a duel. When the cows are released to graze, the girls and boys pour water under the duel to cool the ground.

The young men and women who are fattening rest in duel on their papyrus mats throughout the day, surrounded by food items. Young girls are around to serve the youths if needed. At the end of the six week fattening period, some youths become so fat that they struggle to walk. They end their isolation, returning the milking cows to the cattle camps, and going home to their villages, where they eat their usual food items.

Over the months following the fattening period, the youths gradually lose the weight they have gained. Most will never engage in fattening again, because the necessary food and sacrifices make it very costly, and fattening means that milking cows must be taken away from the young and old, who deserve to be given first priority.

Jieng people have some of the most elaborate marriages in the Republic of South Sudan. The relatives of the bride and the bride-groom spend several days discussing wei (shares of cows for each of the bride's family members). During these sessions, both families bring a lot of food, bulls, and goats. Bulls are swapped, and at the end of each day, bulls are slaughtered for feasts.

In Jieng families, a group of people who share one great ancestor is referred to as a *kuat* or mac. Husbands and other family heads of a kuat or mac are responsible for the unit's affairs. If there is a problem facing the *kuat*, the son of the eldest male in the group calls a meeting, where all the men search for a solution.

Common *kuat* problems include disputes over bride price divisions and the equitable sharing of the burden of blood compensation, called *puk e tir.*

Problems arising from the division of bride wealth among the relatives are quite common. Some people take their shares in cows when their nieces marry but refuse to share their own daughters' bride prices with the relatives. These issues can lead to serious fights, even deaths, if not settled properly.

Blood compensation burdens are also cause for significant conflict. When a member of a family kills a person of another clan in a fight, they are required by law to pay around thirty cows to the family of the deceased. However, if the killer is hanged, the price becomes a life for a life. Some brothers may refuse to participate in the payment of blood compensation. If kuat elders are unable to settle these cases, they can be taken to a clan level, where they are enforced by law. All family members are forced to pay their share of the payments, otherwise the relatives of the deceased can take the law into their own hands, killing one of the best young men from the clan of the man who killed their relative.

Men are responsible for negotiating marriages for their daughters and sons. Marrying off daughters is very important. Fathers must consider the number of cows offered as bride price and the quality of husbands they choose for their daughters. Women are never allowed to participate in marriage negotiations; this activity is male domain.

While the mother of the girl getting married gets the maximum share of her bride price—ten cows, called ariek—she has no rights to decide how these cows can be used. The bride mother's husband is responsible for all decisions regarding the cattle.

Fathers and paternal uncles of sons are responsible for approving potential wives. The girl must come from one of an outstanding family, and it is preferred that she has younger siblings.

One of the most contentious issues faced by Jieng women is polygamy. Jieng women have quietly fought against this tradition for many centuries without success.

The paramount chiefs of many Jieng communities in the former Bhar-el-Ghazal province are polygamists. These chiefs have many wives—sometimes thirty, forty or even seventy—and many subsequent children. These paramount chiefs represent the richest class of their communities, just like the rich class in the Western world. The Jieng philosophy is that being wealthy in people—wives and children—and cattle is the best position one can dream for their life. Women do not often like the idea of sharing their husbands, but because women are culturally dominated in Jieng communities, there is little they can do about it.

Polygamy has survived for centuries, because the system is land-based. That is, each woman has her own homestead, where her house is built and the surrounding land is hers to cultivate her food crops. This means that each wife produces her own food. Some men can cover a whole area as a village for themselves, having so many houses, each for a different wife. Some urban polygamous men acquire land in rural areas to build houses for their wives where there is space to farm. While the men stay with one wife in town, the rest cultivate crops for their families in the villages. The women swap places periodically, so that each wife has a chance to spend time staying with the husband in town. Polygamy is not very popular among urban people, because most urban people are educated and many are Christians, whose faith prevents them from having multiple wives.

One of the biggest problems with polygamy is that polygamous families are plagued with conflicts between wives called *diar muooc*. This is the hatred between wives married by one man. Sometimes, this hatred is so intense that one woman kills a co-wife if the husband does not intervene promptly. If the husband is not a strong personality, each of his families remains an island, each woman and her children separate from her co-wives and their children in all but their shared husband and last name.

Polygamy is not the creation of the Jieng community alone. It has existed in all human communities throughout the world and is still prevalent in many cultures today. Rates of polygamy have decreased, however, in much of the developed world. There are many reasons for this.

Polygamy is an economic burden. With the exception of very rich people, many urban people are unable to afford to support large or multiple families. In Jieng and other South Sudanese tribes, systems of polygamy are likely to disappear as education and urbanisation increase.

One of the positives of polygamy is that it provides marriage to women who might not otherwise be able to find it. Most women in Jieng society get married, unlike in the Western World, where some women remain unmarried all their lives. The population of women is greater than that of men, so when men are restricted to marrying one woman only, there is a surplus of women left unwed. In polygamous societies like Jieng, men are able to marry multiple wives, reducing the impact of population discrepancies. More women are able to marry husbands and start families, and larger familial networks can be created by the joining of multiple or shared families.

CHAPTER SIX

When a Woman Becomes Old

Menopause signals the arrival of a woman's old age and typically occurs when a woman is between forty-five and fifty years old, though there are exceptions, and rarely, women have produced babies at fifty years and older.

In Jieng communities, when women are still strong in their fifties and early sixties, they usually stay at cattle camps, looking after their grandchildren. At this stage of life, women are completely free from household responsibilities, which now belong to the younger generation of women.

At cattle camps, older women drink a lot of milk and, if there are many milking cows, they make *ghee*. Milk is put into a large gourd container and covered with a lid, then shaken to separate the cream from the milk. This is called *mok e gom* or *bi gom muok*. In the evenings, women skim off the cream, which is cooked to make *ghee*. The remaining skimmed milk can be mixed with fresh milk and drunk or eaten with acida.

While at cattle camps taking care of their grandchildren, the grandmothers are visited regularly by their daughters and daughters-in-in law, who bring them food supplies and tobacco products from home.

When women are between sixty-five and seventy years old, they are brought to the villages, usually to one of their daughters' houses. Women of this age are often weak and have blurred eyesight. If enough cows are available, a milking cow is brought to the house to provide a continuous supply of fresh milk. Old women are cared for by their children. Women of this age are often visited by their relatives, who praise them greatly for their services to their families and the community.

There are old Jieng women who lack families to praise and care for them, but even these women become symbols of fame and power in their communities. Girls of marriageable age and young producing mothers come to serve and ask advice of elderly women. They ask the women to put their hands on their heads, blessing them for their own journeys to old age. Members of the community tell stories of the old women's positive deeds, and young girls aim to emulate them.

Old women are widely respected and are fondly called 'Grandma' by most. Grandmas teach children and young people the stories of old ancestors and family trees, singing ancestral lines for children to memorise. Elderly women are often turned to for opinions, ideas, and memories, asked to clarify issues from earlier years and looked to for sage advice on family issues.

When a woman becomes very old and approaches death, she calls for her children, especially the girls. She tells them that the time is coming for her to join her ancestors and says, 'Listen carefully to these words. You, all my children, both boys and girls, you must love one another. If one of you is in trouble and needs help, the others must all rush to your aid. Girls, you must love your brothers; they depend on you and your bride price for their wives. Once you are married to a man, make sure that you hold him with both your hands and be his wife forever, unless something really drastic happens to separate you from him. The idea of having *buong karou* will not be tolerated.

'And boys," the woman says, 'your father was a well-known man in this community. He spoke the truth and performed commendable deeds. Follow in the footsteps of your father, and don't do anything that will make the community dislike you and tarnish his good name and standing.

'Now, when the time comes for me to pass away, don't waste your time on crying, because I am dying of old age, and instead of crying, you should be thankful to God for allowing me to do all that I did. Kill any number of animals you wish to upon my grave. Rejoice and praise the Lord Almighty.'

Old men follow similar practices for death. But dying elderly people rarely realise that the world they are leaving will change drastically after they are gone from it. Time will bring new environments, mindsets, and practices. Foreign cultures will influence and reshape traditions.

Once, traditional Jieng people used spears and clubs for fighting. In those days, it was abominable to commit theft or to kill a person, unless that person or their relative had killed a family member. Stalking an enemy and killing them was and is considered an act of cowardice in Jieng culture. Brave men alert their enemies, allowing them to prepare themselves, meaning that if they are killed, they die knowing that they have been defeated by a stronger opponent.

There are other types of enmity practices in Jieng culture that don't include killing. Instead, a man lets his opponent live to look forward to their next fight. If he hasn't heard from his enemy in some time, he might begin to get worried and send a word to ask how his enemy is faring. If he hears that his enemy is dead, he mourns, because no one remains with whom he can continue this benign enmity.

Jieng culture has changed significantly over the course of the last century, and the wisdom of many dying ancestors is not applicable to modern times. Jieng people have been influenced greatly by foreign ideas. They have become terribly materialistic. Guns have reached Jieng territory following the war of liberation. Jieng sections now conduct cattle raids on other sections, resulting in the unnecessary looting and killing of youths, social instability and disorganisation leading to disrupted local food production, and deaths of young people. Theft is today committed shamelessly. Divorce has increased dramatically, and some people want Jieng society to mirror the Western world in its prevalence. People have lost their grip on morality and societal norms and values, leading to the degradation of humanity.

Westernisation has had a huge impact on the lives of Jieng people. Many have travelled to Europe, Australia, and the United States, and they have brought Western values and practices back to their Jieng tribes. Women who have stayed in Western countries have adopted Western styles of living, beginning to disobey their husbands and fight against cruelty, even leaving their husbands to remarry or live as single mothers.

Old, revered traditions of respect for elders have begun to disappear, and the opinions of old men are now less valued than ever. It is hoped that better times are coming for Jieng communities and that people will be reminded of their cultural roots.

CHAPTER SEVEN

The Impact of Foreign Cultures on Jieng Culture

O ver the millennia, many different types of foreigners have tried to enter Jieng territory by sea, land, and through the River Nile. One such nation was Rome.

Between the years 62 and 67AD, Emperor Nero sent a small expedition to explore the sources of the Nile in an attempt to gather information that would help him to conquer Ethiopia. But instead of sailing down the Blue Nile, the crew mistakenly sailed down the White Nile, and as they progressed southwards, they were blocked by the Sudd north of Malakal.

The Sudd is a fetid wetland filled with ferns, papyrus reeds, and thick mats of rotten vegetation that has been untouched for millions of years. During the rainy seasons, it covers a very large area, larger than England, becoming a vast humid swamp full of crocodiles, hippos, and mosquitoes. The Sudd forms a complete barrier to any form of navigation. It is considered a natural general, like the Russian winter that saved Moscow when foreigners wanted to invade.

Other foreigners tried to reach Jieng territory from the East

African coast through Mombasa. These people were traders from Yemen, Oman, Persia, India, Malaysia, and China.

The Omani Sultanate established the Zanj Empire in the nineteenth century on the East African coast, centred in Zanzibar Island, for the sole purpose of conducting slave-trade activities. They acquired many slaves from East Africa, South Sudan's Equatoria Province, and even Jieng territory, despite its distance from the coast. The invaders suffered heavy losses from their contact with the locals, who could not easily be seen, because they ran into the thick forests.

The prevailing military strategy of the Jieng people was to kill or disable the invaders' horses, depriving the invaders of transport. Then, they could attack and kill the invaders. Foreign invasions soon stopped in Jieng territory, much to the relief of the locals.

The next wave of foreigners to reach South Sudan and Jieng territory were the Turks. Mehmed II conquered Constantinople (now called Istanbul) in 1453 and founded the Ottoman Empire. By the sixteenth century, the Empire had reached its zenith, covering a vast area of northern Africa. The Empire was divided into provinces, each one ruled by a governor appointed by authorities in Constantinople.

In 1821, the Ottoman Empire, under orders of its Egyptian Government, invaded northern Sudan. The Empire remained in Sudan until 1885, when General Gordon was beheaded by Mahdi on 25 January, ending what had come to be known in Sudan as the Turkiyya period.

Invaders established themselves in Khartoum with a small outpost in Juba. One of the reasons for acquiring this new territory was to obtain a steady supply of slaves for the Ottoman Empire. Authorities in Khartoum organised the local Arab population into a militia, which conducted raids in South Sudan to find slaves. All parts of South Sudan were affected by these slave raids.

When Zubeir Pasha was made the Governor of Bhar-el-Ghazal, slave raids increased substantially in the area. The local Fertid tribes suffered greatly. The Jieng areas were affected by increased attacks, and though they fought bravely to protect themselves and their property, raiders took a good number of them as slaves, especially from northern areas. In Eastern Bhar-el-Ghazal, in what is now Lakes region, attacks intensified, and many locals were taken as slaves.

The raiders built a slave centre in what is today called Pendit, a few kilometres north of the current Rumbek City. They chose high ground and built a moat for defence purposes. They crafted a movable bridge from bamboo, which they pulled away at night.

Wuol Athian, from a northern part of Western Lakes State called Pakam Wuol (named in his honour) organised for local Agaar youths to attack the slave centre. First, they measured the width of the moat. Then, Wuol organised the fighters into groups of five hundred. Each group was to bring three hundred tall logs from nearby ameth trees and help make a number of instant bridges across the moat.

The groups approached the centre stealthily to launch a surprise attack. They dropped the logs to make temporary bridges, and they crossed quickly to attack the raiders with their spears in the wee hours of the morning.

The raiders used old guns that had to be cleaned after they'd been fired. This meant that the attacking Jieng had time to move and kill the raiders as they cleaned their guns. Jieng people overran the centre and freed captured slaves, killing so many raiders in the process that only a few escaped alive.

The Turkish militia did not return to Rumbek until the end of slave trade. The slave centre remains intact today, now filled with mud and other debris.

Attacks continued intermittently throughout South Sudan for almost half a century until 1896, when the British Government ended slave trade worldwide.

By the nineteenth century, the Ottoman Empire became 'a sick man of Europe,' and several of its provinces had broken away and formed different dynasties and independent countries. One of those provinces was Egypt, whose governor, Muhammad Ali Pasha, made his province into a kingdom and called himself the Khedive of Egypt. With the British Government's approval, the Khedive of Egypt appointed Major General Charles Gordon as Governor General of Sudan in 1873. Sudan at this time was occupied by Egypt.

Sudan was also invaded by British forces. After a decisive victory over the Egyptian forces in September 1882, the British occupied Sudan and controlled its government. From 1882 until 1922, Britain occupied Egypt as a veiled protectorate. Rising to international recognition, Muhammad Ahmed El Mahdi staged a serious revolt and besieged Khartoum until the city fell on 25 January 1885. General Gordon was beheaded, and his head was taken to Al Mahdi, ending the Turkish/Egyptian rule in Sudan.

This angered Britain, because Charles Gordon was a British citizen in the service of the Khedive. Since Britain was in control of Egyptian affairs, it decided to invade Sudan and punish the dervishes, the Mahdists (or Ansar), who established the first Islamic Government in Sudan.

General Lord Kitchener was appointed the commanding general of the invading army and assembled a militia of around fifty-two thousand men from Egypt, Austria, Sudan, and Britain. In early 1898, they began to move towards Sudan, building railways. By 2 September 1898, the two armies met at Jebel Kerreri, eleven miles north of Omdurman.

British forces conquered the Ansar, the army of Abdullahi Al-Taaisha, who was the successor to the proclaimed Mahdi, Muhammad Ahmad, whose army was almost twice that of the British. Lord Kitchener marched into Omdurman and claimed the new territory for Britain, thus beginning Anglo-Egyptian Sudan, or Anglo-Egyptian Condominium, whereby Sudan was ruled by Britain and Egypt.

However, the conquest of the new territory was not complete until the Battle of Umm Diwaykarat, which was fought on 25 November

1899 in Kordofan, where Abdullahi had run with the remnants of his forces after his defeat in Omdurman. This was the final defeat of the Mahdi forces by General Wingate, who was commanding the British army that went there. Knowing that all was over, Khalifa Abdullahi sat down with his generals and waited to be executed. The Anglo-Egyptian Sudan was a misnomer. Though Egyptians were granted minor roles as clerks and administrators, Britain was the real ruler and coloniser of Sudan.

In January 1899, Lord Kitchener was appointed the first governor general of Sudan. In December 1899, he was summoned to South Africa and succeeded by Reginald Wingate. Wingate would become the longest ruling governor general in history and would be responsible for determining the borders of modern Sudan. He swapped Gambela with Kassala, cutting some of the Nuer people to Ethiopia. The territory was divided into nine provinces—six in the North and three in the South—and the British remained in Sudan for a further fifty-seven years, meaning that Sudan was ruled by foreigners for a total of one hundred and twenty-one years.(64 years of the Turks and 57 years of British)

When the British left Sudan in 1956, some people from the North, who claimed to be Arabs, wanted to dominate the South, replacing the British as colonial masters. In actual fact, these were the mixed-race Afro-Arab products of Arab men from the Arabian Peninsula with the local black women whom they had married.

The South revolted, and after half a century of upheaval and instability in Sudan, the South finally got its independence through a referendum in 2011, by which time political instability had led many South Sudanese people to leave their country, emigrating to countries around the world.

Contact with foreign cultures shook Jieng culture and the cultures of other South Sudanese tribes to their very foundations. The introduction of education and formal religion (Christianity) altered Jieng society greatly, changing mindsets and ways of thinking and living.

Once, Jieng people did not appreciate the idea of education for girls, only allowing boys to go to school. Now, it is far more common for girls to attend schools, because Jieng people have seen the importance and value of girls' education, and their attitudes have shifted.

The introduction of law, order, and formal government was a significant change for an area that had never witnessed such things before. In traditional South Sudanese societies, there was no formal government system as such, but there was a veiled government in the form of a committee of older men, some of whom were spiritual leaders, who made decisions on issues that affected society as a whole.

The Colonial Administration was well-organised. At the head was the Governor General, the chairman of the executive council. The council included civil, legal, financial, and defence secretaries, an inspector general of police, a military commander, and four other British officials. The Governor General appointed provincial governors to rule the provinces on his behalf.

In the provinces, there were two sets of courts. Traditional courts worked with traditional culture, values, norms, and senses of justice and were usually manned by local traditional chiefs appointed by the district commissioner. New courts represented the English legal system and were manned by educated men and women called lawyers, who were posted to provincial and district headquarters all over the country.

Colonial administration established a very effective law and order system that brought general peace to South Sudan, abolishing traditional legal systems that were based on vendetta systems, cycles of violence, and strength that allowed strong men to impose their own laws. Mindsets changed, and crime was more greatly discouraged by the threat of justice instituted by the authorities.

Thanks must be given where it is due, so South Sudan thanks the British Colonial Administration for establishing such an effective legal system that brought unprecedented peace for a period of fifty-seven years. Sadly, this system was discontinued when the Republic of South Sudan won its independence in 2011. It has been replaced by unprecedented chaos and lawlessness, with malfunctioning and corrupt law enforcement agencies unable to restore order.

Before the British came, the economy of Jieng, like the rest of South Sudan, was based on a bartering system. With the arrival of the British, money was introduced for the first time. Now, all South Sudanese people, including Jieng, value money, making people very materialistic. Most Jieng people today prefer money to cows.

Introduced legal systems, education, and money have fundamentally changed almost everything in all of Africa's traditional communities, including Jieng and other traditional tribes in South Sudan. South Sudanese people in the diaspora are most affected, especially those born in foreign countries. Some of these people are beginning to view important traditional values and norms negatively. They think that bride prices are misogynistic and unethical, equivalent to selling girls. And in South Sudan, girls are increasingly being allowed to make their own choices for marriage in the educated class living in urban areas. It is only a matter of time before all girls will be able to choose their own husbands without any relative input.

CHAPTER EIGHT

Concluding Remarks

This book is about how Jieng society perceives women and their place in society. To Jieng people, women are at the centre of everything, allowing society to run smoothly. Women provide child-bearing and rearing, household and care services, and bride prices for their families.

Jieng women are often brutally treated if they do not conform to cultural norms and traditions, and the majority of Jieng people, women included, are unaware that women's rights are being violated. Most people think that training, violence, and restrictions are for the good of women and society as a whole.

In Jieng culture, like in the cultures of other African tribes, people perceive women as weaker and lower than men. This idea is taught to young girls early in life, leading them to believe it wholeheartedly as adults, but it is not true all the time; strong women exist in South Sudan.

Jieng girls are not free to choose their own husbands. Female Jieng revolutionaries have rebelled against this for centuries with little progress. Now, through education, attitudes are changing among Jieng people. The educated classes are allowing their girls to choose their own spouses, and more and more women are marrying for love. One day, hopefully soon, this will become common practice in all Jieng communities.

Jieng people see girls as opportunities for wealth, and they remain uncomfortable with the idea of sending them to unknown educational institutions, where they will learn what Jieng elders do not understand. Elders fear that girls who are taught new ideas will reject the Jieng way of life, so they refuse to send their girls to school.

But it is becoming apparent that education can benefit girls, their families, and society at large. Educated families now embrace education for girls. In rural areas, pockets of resistance to girls' education remain, but in time, female education will be accepted by all.

Marrying a wife in Jieng communities involves paying between thirty and four hundred cows. Jieng men in the diaspora often pay A$70,000 for their brides. Materialism has escalated. These changes cause problems, because these excessively high bride prices exclude men who have no cattle or money, leaving them to remain without wives. This prevents communities from growing. Jieng society must establish fair systems that allow the majority of its citizens to access important community activities and traditions. A moratorium on bride price is becoming necessary.

Violence against wives by their husbands and against daughters by their bothers is today so prevalent that it is accepted as normal. In fact, some women are so used to being victims of domestic violence that they deliberately provoke attacks if they are not regular, fearful that not being beaten means that they are doing something wrong. Fortunately, this expectation is changing, particularly among educated women.

Women in Jieng communities are overworked, still subscribing to traditional duty divisions that are centuries old. But lifestyle, culture, and environment have changed, so practices and duties should follow. Transitions must be gradual in order to avoid male backlash.

In urban areas and towns, cooking has been modernised and

simplified. Husbands and sons should begin to help women wash dishes, shop for food items, cook meals, and clean homes.

In rural areas, boys' education has altered traditional roles, including cattle care and war training. Boys should now be taught how to clean houses, sweep compounds, and fetch firewood alongside their sisters. These small changes will path the way for bigger changes in the future.

School curriculum can help to reshape gender bias, educating children on changing gender roles and responsibilities.

Women are a part of all Jieng culture. It is time they are respected for their value.

NB: An interesting story of a woman beating up her man, and when the neighbours arived she was found having put herself under the man, pretending that she was the one who had been beaten to confirm the cultural myth that men are generally stronger than women. This story is of great interest and value to women on their way to mental recovery as normal human beings, instead of always believing themselves as eternally weak which is not naturally true.

Acknowledgements

In 1971, I was pursuing my Master's degree in Agricultural Economics at Oregon State University. I had an argument with a Ghanaian colleague called Seth about the trading of raw agricultural products, such as coffee beans, without any form of processing.

Many less developed countries (LDCs) sell their unprocessed agricultural products to industrialised countries at a fraction of their true value. There, the products are processed, and the LDCs then buy them back at more than three times their raw-state value. We call this economic colonisation or neo-colonisation. In order to benefit financially from their own products, LDCs must introduce some form of processing to add value to products before they are exported.

I explained this to Seth, and he looked at me and asked, "Have you ever thought about writing a book?"

I hadn't.

"You'd better," Seth told me. "You are so lucid.".

My dear wife, too, has been telling me all our married life, since 31 June 1985, that I should write books on the important social issues I care so deeply about.

I have been reflecting on these comments, and I have been doing a lot of research. Over the next couple of years, I aim to write and publish books about agricultural economics, outlining the importance of using economic principles to conduct effective trade amidst agricultural problems, using the Republic of South Sudan as my analytic focus.

The encouragement of my graduate students, my colleagues, and my family has given me more impetus to think about the art of writing. I have registered at an institution that teaches writing skills and aim to use what I learn to produce better writing and better books.

When I discovered a publishing company owned by and working to publish and promote South Sudanese talent, I knew I had found my publisher, one who would respect my voice and story.

Peter Deng of Africa World Books was friendly and enthusiastic about my story of escape from Sudan. He had heard my name before and could discuss my manuscript with me in our local language. He asked me to submit my story, one of my proudest moments, and the rest is history.

I encourage all budding authors who want to write positively about South Sudan to contact Peter Deng by email at info@africa-worldbooks.com or by phone on 0422 611 978.

I thank Peter Deng and Africa World Books for believing in and publishing my story. I hope that many more authors can embrace the support of Africa World Books as they share their stories of South Sudan with the world.

I thank my daughters, Sarah, Ayola, and Alawen, and my dear wife, Priscilla Akol, for helping me to achieve my writing dreams.

I thank the traditional African chiefs in Australia for their commitment to maintaining cultures and traditions. I honour Sultan Aleer Gatluak Deng Athoi, who was the first South Sudanese man to be made a chief in the diaspora, and Peter Lual Reech Deng, the Twic East acting Chief—Lual established the Foundation for Traditional Council for Chiefs to regulate dowry practice and conflict resolution and to help maintain South Sudanese culture in Australia.

This book will support service providers, young people, and traditional chiefs in revising the cultures and traditions of the past.

Dedication

This book is dedicated to all those brave girls, like Muona, who have fought indefatigably over the centuries for the right to choose their lovers and not to be given to men they do not love. Although they have not achieved much, their efforts will ultimately bring fruitful results when most Jieng people become educated.

Sultan Aleer Galuak Deng

Sultan Peter Lual Reech Deng

Prof Dr Daniel A Mamer the author.

Acknowledgement

Special thanks go to the South Sudanese Community Association leaders in various states across Australia and to the professions, service providers and Government agencies for their good work.

Akuot Aciek Akuot of the South Sudan Community Association of Western Australia Inc. has done exceptionally well with his teams.